Dave Lambert

Oh, Oscar!

Two short plays

Ernst Klett Verlag
Stuttgart München Düsseldorf Leipzig

Dieses Werk folgt im Deutschen der reformierten Rechtschreibung.

Zu dieser Lektüre gibt es eine Kassette (Klettnummer 572221).

Gedruckt auf Recyclingpapier, hergestellt aus 100% Altpapier.

1. Auflage 1 5 4 3 2 1 | 2001 00 1999 1998 1997

Alle Drucke dieser Auflage können im Unterricht nebeneinander benutzt werden. Die letzte Zahl bezeichnet das Jahr dieses Druckes.

Zeichnungen: Elsie Lennox, London.
Druck: Wilhelm Röck, Weinsberg. Printed in Germany.

ISBN 3-12-572220-9

Contents

Oscar Goes Babysitting

List of characters

Oscar
Mr and Mrs Wilson
Jake, their two-year-old son
Gran, his grandmother
Nick, Oscar's friend
Lucy, Nick's sister
Constable 1
Constable 2
Woman in a red coat

4 **Gran** Oma, Großmutter
7 **constable** ['kʌnstəbl] Polizist/in

Scene One

Oscar is babysitting for the Wilsons. They are going out for the evening. He must look after Jake, their two-year-old son. Jake's Gran also lives in the house. At the beginning of the play they are all in the kitchen.

Mrs Wilson: Mr Wilson and I are going to the theatre, Oscar. Are you sure you will be OK with Jake? He's had his bath.

Oscar: This is the first time I've babysat, Mrs Wilson, but I'm sure Jake will be fine with me!

Mrs Wilson: You see, Gran usually babysits. But she can't now.

Gran: No, I can't walk upstairs to put Jake to bed. I'm too old!

Mr Wilson: But Gran will be in the living-room, Oscar.

Gran: If you need anything, Oscar, just ask me!

Oscar: Thanks! Don't worry, I can put Jake to bed.

Gran: Oh, good. I'll just go into the living-room then. There's an old film I want to see on TV. It's called '*Kidnapped*'. Some terrible men kidnap a young boy and take him on a boat. It's very good ...

1 **to go out**	ausgehen
13 **to put a child to bed**	ein Kind ins Bett bringen
22 *Kidnapped*	Roman von R.L. Stevenson
23 **to kidnap** ['--], **kidnapped**	entführen

(Gran goes into the living-room.)

Mrs Wilson: You'll hear Jake if he cries, won't you Oscar?

Oscar: Oh yes, I'll hear him, Mrs Wilson! I'll just sit here at the kitchen table and do my homework.

Mr Wilson: I'm sure Oscar and Jake will be fine, dear. Come on, we'll be late for the theatre.

Mrs Wilson: Oh, Oscar, I've made a chocolate cake. It's in the fridge. Just help yourself! But don't give Gran any cake. It's not good for her!

Mr Wilson: No, the doctor says she mustn't eat sweet things. But she likes them so much! *(They all laugh.)*

Mr and Mrs Wilson: Goodbye Jake! Goodbye Oscar!

Oscar and Jake: Bye bye! Bye bye!

(Mr and Mrs Wilson leave.)

Oscar: Come on, Jake. Upstairs! Time for bed!

(Oscar takes Jake upstairs and puts him to bed.)

Oscar's voice: Goodnight, Jake! Sleep tight!. Sssshhh!

Jake's voice: 'Night! 'Night!

10	**fridge** [frɪdʒ]	Kühlschrank
10	**Just help yourself!**	bediene dich, bitte!
14	**she likes them so much**	sie isst sie so gern
22	**Sleep tight** [taɪt]!	schlafe gut/fest!
23	**'night = goodnight**	Gute Nacht

(Oscar comes back downstairs into the kitchen. He stops and listens by the living-room door.)

Oscar: Hmmm .... She's watching that old film, 'Kidnapped' ... I'm hungry! Ah! There's a chocolate cake in the fridge. (*He opens the fridge.*) Mmmmm! I think I'll have a piece!

(He takes the cake out and puts it on the kitchen table. He cuts a big piece. He sits down at the kitchen table with his back to the living-room door.)

Oscar: Aaaah! Babysitting is so easy! I'll do my homework later .... (*He has an idea.*) I know! I'll phone my friends Nick and Lucy! (*He picks up the phone. Speaking with his mouth full of cake*) Hello, Nick!

Nick: Hello ...? Who's that?

Oscar: It's me! Oscar!

Nick: Oscar, are you eating?

Oscar: Yeah, I am. Chocolate cake! I'm babysitting for the Wilsons.

Nick: All by yourself?

Oscar: No, Jake's Gran's here but she can't walk upstairs. She's watching an old film in the living-room ...

Nick: How much do you get for babysitting, Oscar?

20 **yeah** [jeə] (*informal*) ja
22 **all by yourself** ganz allein

Oscar: One fifty an hour! I can buy that new skateboard soon!

Nick: Wow! Lucky you, Oscar! I'm just doing my homework ...

Oscar: Homework's boring! I've got my walkman, so I can listen to that new CD I bought last Saturday ... Heavy Metal!

Nick: But Oscar, you can't listen to that ...

Oscar: Why not? It's cool! (*Oscar starts to sing.)* Naaaa ... Naaaa ... Naaaaa!!

Nick: But if Jake cries ...?

Oscar: What? Sorry, Nick, I must go. It's time for another piece of chocolate cake!

(He puts the phone down and takes another piece of cake.)

Mmmm! Babysitting is so easy! (*listens*) I can't hear Jake! Fast asleep already!

(He puts his earphones in his ears and puts his feet up on the table. His mouth is full of chocolate cake and his eyes are closed. He is singing. Jake comes into the kitchen behind Oscar. He is crying.)

Jake: I want my Mummy!

(Oscar does not hear him. Jake stands in front of him but Oscar's eyes are closed.)

1 **one fifty an hour** (£1.50)	ein Pfund fünfzig pro Stunde
3 **Lucky** [ʌ] **you!**	Du Glückspilz!
17 **to be fast asleep**	tief/fest schlafen
18 **earphones**	Kopfhörer

Oscar: (*singing*) Naaa ... naaaa ... Naaaaa!

Jake: (*loud*) I want my Mummy!!

Oscar: (*singing*) Naaaa ... Naaaaa ... NAAAA!

Jake: (*very loud*) I want my Mummy! Waaahhh! Waaahhh! I want my Mummy!

(Gran comes into the kitchen behind Oscar.)

Gran: What's all the noise? I can't hear my film! (*She sees Jake.*) Jake! Come to Gran! What's wrong? Gran's here!

Jake: Gran!

(He goes to Gran.)

Gran:	(*behind Oscar*) Well, really! What kind of a babysitter are you, Oscar Beaton?! You sit there and do nothing when little Jake is crying!

(Oscar cannot hear Gran. He is listening to his music. Gran stands in front of him but Oscar's eyes are closed.)

Gran:	Well, Oscar? .... I'm waiting for an answer!
Oscar:	(*singing with his eyes closed*) Naaaa ... Naaaaa ... Naaaaa!
Gran:	(*Gran sees the earphones.*) Oh, Oscar! How can you hear Jake with those things in your ears? Come on, Jake. You can come in the living-room with me and sleep on the sofa.

(Gran sees the chocolate cake on the table. She takes a big piece. Oscar does not see her.)

Jake:	(*happy*) Chocolate! Chocolate!
Gran:	Ssssh! Jake! Don't tell anyone! No one will know. (*She laughs.*)

(She gives Jake a piece of cake, then takes him into the living-room and closes the door.)

Oscar:	(*taking his earphones out*) Fantastic music! (*singing*) Naaa ... Naaaaa ... Naaaa ...

1	**Well, really!**	also, wirklich!
1	**What kind** [aɪ] **of a ...?**	was für ein/eine/einen ...?
15	**sofa** [ˈsəʊfə]	Sofa, Couch

(He stops. He looks at the chocolate cake.)

Oscar: *(surprised)* Gosh! Have I eaten so much chocolate cake ...? There's only one piece left! Hmm ... I can't hear Jake. He must be fast asleep. Hmmm ... I'll just go upstairs and see ...

(He goes upstairs.)

Oscar's voice: Oh no! Jake? Jake? Where are you? Jake!! Jake!! JA-KEY!

(He comes back down. His face is white. He looks under the table. He opens some cupboards and looks inside. Then he makes a terrible face and looks in the fridge.)

Oscar: Oh no! What can I do? I know, I'll tell Jake's Gran ... but if she tells the Wilsons I lost Jake, I'm in big trouble! Oh ... Nick ... I'll phone Nick!

(He picks up the telephone.)

Nick? Oooooh, Nick! You must help me!

Nick: Have you eaten too much chocolate cake, Oscar?

Oscar: No! It's Jake! He's ... he's gone!

2 **surprised** [sə'praɪzd] überrascht
2 **so much** so viel
4 **one piece left** ein Stück übrig
15 **to lose, lost, lost** verlieren

Nick: What do you mean 'he's gone'?

Oscar: I put him to bed upstairs ... and now he isn't there! Mr and Mrs Wilson will kill me!

Nick: But he must be somewhere in the house, Oscar! Lucy and I will come over and look for him!

(Oscar puts the telephone down. He walks up and down the kitchen. He looks under the table again. There is a knock at the door. Oscar opens it. Nick and Lucy come into the kitchen.)

Nick: I thought you said babysitting was so easy, Oscar.

Lucy: Jake must be somewhere in the house, Oscar ...

Oscar: I've looked everywhere! He's gone! Ooooh!

Nick: (*going to the living-room door*) Have you looked in the living-room?

Oscar: No! Don't go in there! Jake's Gran's in there!

Lucy: Well, we must tell her!

Oscar: No! If she knows I've lost Jake, I'm in big trouble! Jake can't be in there!

Nick: Well, we'll look upstairs. He's probably just hiding under his bed!

(Nick and Lucy go upstairs.)

3 **to kill** umbringen
6 **to come over** herüberkommen
10 **there is a knock** es klopft
16 **everywhere** ['evrɪweə] überall

Oscar: (*looking in the cupboards*) The Wilsons will kill me! (*looking under the table*) How will I get enough money to buy that new skateboard now?

(*He looks out the kitchen window into the street.*)

Oscar: Ooooh! What ...? That woman ... she's got a little boy with her! She's putting him in her car! But that's ... that's Jake! Oh no! She's *kidnapping* Jake! She's driving away! Stop! Stop! ... The number! ... I'll take the number!

(*He writes the number of the car on a piece of paper.*)

Oscar: (*shouts*) Nick! Lucy! (*remembering*) Oh! I mustn't shout. Gran will hear!

(Nick and Lucy come back in.)

Oscar: (*pointing*) That white car! ... That woman!

Nick: What white car?

Lucy: What woman? (*They run to the window and look into the street.)*

Oscar: She's ... kidnapped ... Jake!!

Nick and Lucy: Kidnapped !?

Oscar: Yes! She put him in her car and drove away with him.

Lucy: Is this one of your jokes, Oscar?

Oscar: I'm not joking! Look I've got the number! EDX 181 D.

Nick: You mean she just walked in, went upstairs and kidnapped him from his bed?

Oscar: Yeees!

Lucy: Are you sure that woman had Jake, Oscar?

Oscar: (*angry*) Of course I'm sure!

Nick: Well, now we *must* tell Gran, Oscar!

Oscar: No! This is a job for the police!

(He phones the police.)

4	**to point at s.th.**	auf etwas zeigen
14	**I'm not joking**	ich scherze nicht, es ist kein Scherz
23	**job** [dʒɒb]	*hier*: Aufgabe

Oscar:	(*speaking in a high voice because he is worried*) Hello? Police? Someone has kidnapped little Jake Wilson! You must find him!
Constable's voice:	Good evening, madam. Are you the mother?
Oscar:	No, of course not! I'm the babysitter!
Constable :	Your name?
Oscar:	Oscar Beaton! I saw the woman! She took him and drove away in a white car ... I have the number: EDX 181 D!
Constable :	A white car ... EDX 181 D ...
Oscar:	She had a red coat ... oh, and she had brown hair.
Constable:	What's the address please?
Oscar:	24 Windsor Road.
Constable:	A police car is on its way!

1 **in a high voice**	mit einer hohen Stimme
5 **madam** ['mædəm]	gnädige Frau
15 **address** [-'-]	
17 **on its way**	unterwegs

Scene Two

(There is a knock on the door. The police enter with a woman in a red coat. With her is a small child. He hides his face.)

Constable 1: Good evening. Which of you is Oscar Beaton?

Oscar : I am, Constable!

Constable 2: Have you seen this woman before?

Oscar: Yes, I have, Constable!

Constable 2: Did this woman kidnap Jake Wilson?

Oscar: Yes, she did!

Woman: Oh, no, I didn't!

Constable 1: (*reading*) Brown hair ... red coat ...

Oscar: Yes, that's right, Constable!

Constable 1: (*reading*) White car, number EDX 181 D ...?

Oscar: That's her! .... (*The child turns round.*) B-but ... that's not Jake!!

Constable 2: Not Jake?

Constable 1: If this is a joke, young man, it isn't very funny!

Oscar: It's not a joke, Constable! That's not Jake!

Woman: (*angry*) There, you see! I told you! This is *my* child! I live in this street! I was on my way to the hospital. My child is ill ...

1 **to enter** ['--] eintreten, hereinkommen
25 **on the way to** auf dem Weg nach

Constable 2: Okay, madam. You and your child can go. We're very sorry.

Woman: Huh! Very sorry! Now I'll arrive late at the hospital...

(The woman and her child leave.)

Oscar: I'm sorry, Constable. I ... I thought ...

Constable 1: We know what you thought, Oscar.

Constable 2: You know, you're too young to babysit, Oscar. Is there anyone else in the house?

Oscar: No! ... Er ... Well, yes ... but, you see ...

(The living-room door opens and Gran comes out.)

Gran: What's all the noise about? Why are the police here, Oscar?!

Oscar: Er ... They ... er ...

Constable 1: Somebody has kidnapped Jake Wilson, madam.

Gran: Kidnapped!? ... What are you talking about?

Lucy: Oscar saw a woman in a red coat ...

Nick: And a white car ...

Gran: A woman? A white car? What are you all talking about?

Oscar: She kidnapped Jake!

Gran: Nonsense! Jake is in the living-room! He's fast asleep!

24 **Nonsense!** [ˈnɒnsəns] Quatsch! Unsinn!

(They all look into the living-room. Jake is asleep on the sofa.)

Oscar, Nick, and Lucy: JAKE!

Nick: He was in the living-room all the time!

Gran: Well, of course he was! Kidnapped!?!

Lucy: Fast asleep on the sofa! We told you to look there, Oscar!

Constable 2: Oh, Oscar!! ... Well, we must go now. (*to Oscar*) But next time, Oscar, think *before* you call the police. Please!

Oscar: Yes, Constable ...

(The police leave.)

5 **all the time** die ganze Zeit

Lucy: Oh, Oscar! You and your imagination!

Nick: Kidnapped! Humph! Come on, Lucy. Let's go home!

Nick and Lucy: Bye!

(Nick and Lucy leave.)

Gran: Oh, Oscar! Why didn't you just tell me?

Oscar: I'm sorry. You see, if Mr and Mrs Wilson find out about this, I can never babysit for them again! ... I'll put Jake back upstairs in his bed before they come home.

(Oscar takes Jake upstairs. When he is gone, Gran takes the last piece of chocolate cake from the table. She eats some of it. Oscar comes in. Gran hides the cake behind her back.)

Oscar: I can't understand it. I didn't hear Jake cry ... And I didn't see him go into the living-room ...

Gran: Of course you didn't, Oscar! You had these on! (*She picks up the earphones from the table.*) And your eyes closed!

Oscar : (*sad*) I'm not a very good babysitter, am I? The Wilsons will be very angry ...

Gran: Hmmm ... Well, I won't tell Jake's parents about all this, ... if you don't tell them about the chocolate cake ...

Oscar: Chocolate cake ...? (*He looks at the plate on the table. It is empty now.*) You? ... So that's where it went!

1 **imagination** [ɪˌmædʒɪˈneɪʃn] Fantasie
21 **sad** traurig

Gran: (*showing the piece behind her back*) The doctor says I musn't eat sweet things. But I love chocolate cake!

(Oscar and Gran laugh. Gran puts the last piece of cake in her mouth. Mr and Mrs Wilson come in.)

Mr Wilson: Hello, Oscar! Hello, Gran!
Oscar and Gran: H-h-ello!
Mr Wilson: So, who kidnapped him, Gran?
Gran and Oscar: Wha-at?!
Oscar: W-ho kidnapped who?
Mr Wilson: You know, the boy!
Oscar: *(sad)* So ...y-you know all about it ...?
Mr Wilson: *(surprised)* No, I don't know *anything* about it! That's why I'm asking. Was it good?
Gran: Oh, ... he means the film, Oscar! You know, '*Kidnapped*'! It was good ... very good!
Mrs Wilson: Oh, I see you've eaten all the chocolate cake, Oscar!
Mr Wilson: Well, I hope you didn't have any cake, Gran. You know what the doctor said ...
Gran: Er ... Well ... I ...
Oscar: Oh, no, she didn't! I'm sorry but ... it was so good, I ate it all!
Mrs Wilson: (*surprised*) Well ... I'm glad you liked it, Oscar ...! (*worried*) How was Jake? Any problems?

13 **I don't know anything** ich weiß gar nichts

Oscar: (*looking at Gran*) Jake? P-problems? Well ... er ...

Gran: What problems could there be with a babysitter like Oscar? We had a very quiet evening, didn't we, Oscar?

Oscar: Oh, yes! I just sat here and did all my homework. Very quiet!

THE END

Idee: Dia einer Statue als Hintergrund einblenden

Oscar and the Statue

List of characters

Oscar
Nick
Lucy

Oscar's Mum
Oscar's Dad

Mr Marsh
Constable 1
Constable 2

7 **constable** ['kɒnstəbl] Polizist/in

Scene One: In the garden

Oscar is playing in his back garden with Nick and Lucy.

Nick: Oh, no! The ball's gone over the fence into the neighbour's garden.

Oscar: Now we'll never get it back!

Lucy: Of course, we will, Oscar. We can just ask your neighbour to throw it back.

Oscar: You don't know old Mr Marsh! He doesn't like children in his garden!

Lucy: Well, I'm not scared. I'll climb over the fence and get it ...

(Lucy climbs up and looks over the fence.)

Nick: Can you see the ball, Lucy ?

Lucy: No, I can't. It's a very big garden. Oh, I think I can see your neighbour, Mr Marsh ....

(Nick climbs up next to Lucy to look over the fence.)

Oscar: What's he doing ?

Nick: He's just digging in his garden.

(Oscar climbs up too.)

Oscar: Hmmm ... What's he digging?

2 **fence** [fens]	Zaun
9 **to be scared** [skeəd]	Angst haben
18 **to dig, dug, dug**	(um-)graben

Lucy: A hole, silly! He's probably planting a tree or something.

Oscar: That hole is too big for a tree!

Nick: It is a very big hole .... and it's right in the middle of the garden.

Oscar: Old Marsh is probably burying something secret!

Lucy: Oh, Oscar! You and your imagination!

(Mr Marsh hears the children. He stops and looks around the garden.)

Oscar: He's seen us! Let's get out of here!

(The children climb down and run off.)

1	**to plant**	pflanzen
6	**to bury** ['berı]	begraben
7	**secret** ['si:krıt]	geheim
8	**imagination**	Fantasie, Vorstellungskraft
11	**let's get out of here!**	bloß weg hier!

Scene Two: Robbery at the City Museum

Oscar is doing his homework in the living room. His mum is tidying up and his dad is looking at the newspaper.

Oscar:	Old Mr Marsh next door is digging a big hole in his back garden.
Dad:	Is he?
Oscar:	Yeah, all by himself.
Dad:	He's probably planting a tree or something.
Mum:	He's a little old for that, isn't he? *(to Dad)* Perhaps you could help him, dear?
Dad:	*(looking at his newspaper)* Mmm ....
Oscar:	I don't think he'll want Dad's help, Mum.
Dad:	Why not?
Oscar:	Well, I don't think he's planting a tree. I think he's burying something ...
Mum:	Burying something, Oscar? Like what?
Oscar:	Something secret ... like gold .... or guns maybe!
Dad:	Gold or guns!? Oh, Oscar, you and your imagination!

	robbery	Einbruch
2	**newspaper**	Zeitung
7	**all by himself**	ganz allein
20	**gold** [gəʊld]	
20	**gun** [ʌ]	Gewehr, Pistole

Oscar: Well, I'm sure it's something secret. We can never go into his garden to get our ball. And he was digging until late last night!

Mum: Now, Oscar. That doesn't mean he's burying something secret!

Dad: Oh, dear ... Another robbery in town. This time in the museum ... Listen to this *(reading the newspaper)*: 'Last night thieves stole an Egyptian statue from the City Museum. The statue of Queen Nubia is over two thousand years old ... '

Mum: Two thousand years old ... !

Dad: *(reading)* Hmmm ... It's a heavy statue ... one hundred kilograms. And it's one metre tall ...

Oscar: How did they carry the statue out? There's a big wall around the museum gardens, isn't there?

Dad: *(reading)* Listen! 'The police cannot understand how the thieves got the heavy statue out because there is a wall around the museum gardens. All roads out of the city are closed, so the police

10	**to steal** [iː], **stole, stolen**	stehlen
10	**Egyptian** [ɪ'dʒɪpʃn]	ägyptisch
14	**heavy** ['hevɪ]	schwer
16	**one metre** [iː] **tall** [ɔː]	ein Meter groß
17	**to carry s.th. out**	heraustragen
18	**wall**	Mauer, Wand
21	**to get s.th. out**	herauskriegen

think the thieves are hiding the Egyptian statue somewhere in the city ... '

Mum: Mmmm, yes. If they've closed the roads, it must be in the city.

Oscar: Wow! It could be anywhere!

Dad: *(reading)* Listen to this: 'There is a reward of £5,000 for information about the statue ... '

Oscar: *(looking at the newspaper)* Five thousand pounds?! Can I have your newspaper for a minute, Dad?

Dad: Well ...

Oscar: *(taking the paper)* I'll bring it back ...

(He runs out the front door.)

Dad: My newspaper ... !

Mum: *(surprised)* Oscar! Where are you going? What about your homework?

Dad: What will we do with that boy?!

5 **anywhere** — *hier:* überall
6 **reward** [rɪ'wɔ:d] — Belohnung
16 **surprised** [sə'praɪzd] — überrascht

Scene Three: Oscar finds the thief

Later that evening. Oscar, Nick and Lucy are in Oscar's front garden.

Nick: Five thousand pounds! That's a lot of money, Oscar. Are you sure?

Oscar: It's in the newspaper. Look for yourself if you don't believe me!

Lucy: *(reading)* 'There is a reward of £5,000 for information about the stolen statue ... '

Oscar: You can buy a lot with five thousand pounds!

Lucy: *(still reading)* 'The statue of Queen Nubia is over two thousand years old. It is one metre tall and ... '

Oscar: Hundreds of CDs, thousands of computer games, millions of sweets! We'll be rich! And famous!!

Nick: Yes, Oscar. But we must *find* the statue first ...

Oscar: Ah, but I think I have!

Lucy and Nick: Have what?

Oscar: Found the statue of Queen Nubia!

Lucy: Oh, Oscar! This is one of your silly jokes again!

5 **look for yourself**! schau selber!
6 **to believe** [bɪˈliːv] glauben
14 **hundreds of CDs** Hunderte von CDs
15 **millions** [mɪljənz] **of sweets** Millionen von Bonbons

Oscar:	I'm not joking!
Nick:	Okay then, Oscar. Where is the statue?
Oscar:	Remember that big hole in old Marsh's garden?
Lucy and Nick:	Yeah?
Oscar:	Well, what do you think it's for?
Nick:	Er ... planting a tree?
Oscar:	It's too big for a tree!
Lucy:	Well, ... for burying something?
Oscar:	Exactly! Like the statue of Queen Nubia!
Nick:	Oh, Oscar! You don't really think Mr Marsh ... ?
Oscar:	Oh, yes, I do! Look! There he is!

(They all hide behind tree.)

Nick:	What's he doing?
Lucy:	He's carrying something from his car.
Oscar:	In a wheelbarrow ...
Nick:	A package ...
Lucy:	About one metre tall ...
Oscar:	In brown paper ...
Nick:	And quite heavy ...
Lucy:	Shopping?
Oscar:	That's not shopping! That's the statue of Queen Nubia!!

10 **exactly** [-ˈ--]	genau
18 **wheelbarrow**	Schubkarren
19 **package** [ˈpækɪdʒ]	Paket

Scene Four: In Mr Marsh's garden

Later that evening, in Mr Marsh's garden. Oscar, Lucy and Nick have climbed over the fence.

Lucy:	This is a silly idea, Oscar!
Nick:	He'll probably catch us, Oscar!
Lucy:	And you said Mr Marsh doesn't like children.
Oscar:	Don't worry. We'll just say ... *(thinking)* we've come to get our ball back!

(They walk across Mr Marsh's garden.)

Lucy:	Oh! I almost tripped over that hosepipe!
Nick:	Be careful, Lucy! Don't fall in the hole!
Oscar:	Just look at it! It really is too big to plant a tree ... Come on, you two!
Lucy:	Hey, there's the wheelbarrow!
Oscar:	And the statue of Queen Nubia! Old Marsh has hidden it over by that wall! He probably wants to bury it in the hole later tonight! Then when the police are not looking for it, he'll dig it up and sell it for thousands! Or even millions ...
Nick:	Are you sure it's the statue, Oscar?
Oscar:	Of course it is, silly!
Lucy:	Well, let's take off some of this brown paper so we can see it better ...

(They take some of the brown paper off the statue.)

9	**to walk across**	überqueren
10	**hosepipe** ['həʊzpaɪp]	Schlauch
19	**to dig s.th. up**	etwas ausgraben

Oscar: *(jumping back)* Aaargh!!

Lucy and Nick: Look! It's an eye!

Oscar: It's Queen Nubia's eye! So old Marsh is the thief! Now do you believe me?

Lucy: W-w-what do we do?

Oscar: We tell the police!

Nick: When, now?

Mum's voice: Oscar, where are you? It's late!

Oscar: Oh, there's my mum! *(thinking)* ... We'll tell them tomorrow. It's Saturday, so we can be there when they arrest old Marsh! And get the reward!

Lucy: Are you sure you know what you're doing, Oscar?

Oscar: Of course I do. Just think! We'll be rich! We'll be famous!

11 **to arrest** [-ˈ-] verhaften
16 **famous** [ˈfeɪməs] berühmt

Scene Five: The police arrive

The next day. A police car arrives at Mr Marsh's house. Oscar, Lucy and Nick get out of the car with two police constables. They go to Mr Marsh's front door. They wait a long time before he opens it.

Constable 1:	Good afternoon. Are you James Marsh?
Mr Marsh:	Er ... yes, Constable. I'm sorry I didn't open the door. You see, I was digging in my garden.
Constable 2:	*(interested)* Oh, were you? You spend a lot of time in your garden, don't you?
Mr Marsh:	Yes, I was digging a big hole there.
Constable 1:	(*very interested*) Oh, were you?
Mr Marsh:	But I think I've finished it now.
Constable 2:	Have you, Mr Marsh?
Mr Marsh:	Er ... How can I help you, Constable?
Constable 1:	Can we look in your garden, please?
Mr Marsh:	Y-yes, Constable. But why?
Constable 2:	We think maybe you've got something interesting in it ...
Mr Marsh:	Something interesting?
Constable 1:	Yes. Like a statue, maybe?
Mr Marsh:	Well, yes. I have got a statue ...
Constable 2:	About one metre tall?
Mr Marsh:	Well, yes ... How did you know?
Constable 1:	And quite heavy?

9 **interested** ['ɪntrɪstɪd] interessiert

Mr Marsh: Very heavy! I carried it from the car in a wheelbarrow!

Constable 2: Can we see it?

Mr Marsh: You want to see it? Well, yes ...

(He takes them into his back garden. There is now a beautiful statue and a pond full of water there.)

Mr. Marsh: (*proud*) There she is! It's a copy of the Little Mermaid ... in Copenhagen!

Oscar: *(looking at the statue with big eyes*) The Little Mermaid?!

Mr Marsh: Nice, isn't it? And only £65.95 from the Garden Centre!

7	**proud** [aʊ]	stolz
7	**copy** ['kɒpɪ]	Abbildung, Kopie
8	**mermaid** ['mɜːmeɪd]	Meerjungfrau
11	**£65.95**	sixty-five ninety-five

Oscar: Garden Centre?!

Mr Marsh: It needed a very big hole for the pond. Mermaids like water. Ha. ha!

Constable 2: So you ... haven't got ... an Egyptian statue?

Mr Marsh: Egyptian statue?! No. How much do they cost?

Constable 1: Thank you for your time, Mr Marsh. That's a very beautiful mermaid. And a very nice pond!

(They all leave Mr Marsh's garden.)

Constable 2: (*angry*) This is another one of your mistakes, isn't it, Oscar?

Oscar: I'm ... I'm sorry, Constable. You see,Mr Marsh was digging a big hole and I read in the newspaper about the stolen statue of Queen Nubia. Then we saw him carry something heavy from his car ... in a wheelbarrow! And I thought ... I thought ...

Constable 1: We know what you thought, Oscar! (*thinking*) Hmmm ... But that gives me an idea. (*to Constable* 2) Quick, Constable! Let's go back to the museum!

(The police get in their car and drive away.)

15 **to read, read** [red], **read** lesen

Nick: A stolen Egyptian statue! Ha! It was just a copy of The Little Mermaid!

Lucy: For £65.95 ...

Nick: From the Garden Centre! Ha, ha!

Lucy: “We’ll be rich, we’ll be famous!” That was another one of your brilliant ideas, Oscar!

6 **brilliant** ['brɪljənt] toll, großartig

Scene Six: Rich and famous

Oscar is doing his homework in the living room. His mum is reading a magazine.

Mum: You're very quiet tonight, Oscar. What's wrong?

Oscar: *(sad)* Oh, nothing ...

Mum: Did something happen at school?

Oscar: No ...

(Dad comes in. He is reading the newspaper.)

Dad: Listen! It says here they've found the statue of Queen Nubia.

Oscar: Wha-at ... !?

Dad: Oh, you remember, Oscar. That statue those thieves stole from the City Museum ...

Oscar: Of course, I remember, Dad! But ... but ...

Mum: Where did they find it, dear?

Dad: It says here: 'The police looked everywhere in the city but they could not find the Egyptian statue. No one could understand how the thieves got the heavy statue out because there is a wall around the museum gardens. Then Constable Richard Smith had an idea. They *didn't* get it out. The police found the statue in a hole in the museum gardens ... '

5 **sad** [æ] traurig
17 **everywhere** überall

Oscar: The museum gardens ...?!

Dad: Yes, in a hole. *(reading again)* 'The police are giving a small reward of £300 to a young boy. He helped them find Queen Nubia ... The boy's name is ... ' Huh?!....

Mum: What, dear? Who gets the reward?

Dad: .... 'OSCAR BEATON'?!

Oscar: M-m-me ...?!

Mum: Our Oscar? There must be some mistake!

Dad: *(reading)* 'Constable Smith said: "Oscar's brilliant idea helped us to find the famous statue ... " '

Mum: Oscar? What idea?!

Oscar: Mr Marsh ... the hole ... the mermaid! Oh! I'll tell you later! *(taking Dad's newspaper)* I'm in the newspapers! I'm rich! I'm famous! *(running out with the newspaper)*

Dad: Hey! Come back with my newspaper!

Oscar: I must tell Nick and Lucy!!

Mum and Dad: *(to each other)* What will we do with that boy?!

THE END

Questions and Activities

Oscar Goes Babysitting

Before you read

Talk about:
– your babysitter when you were younger
– the first time you went babysitting
– how much money babysitters can get
– what babysitters must do
– problems for babysitters.

Scene One

Answer these questions:
1. Why can't Gran put Jake to bed?
2. What is the story of '*Kidnapped*'? Have you seen the film or read the book?
3. Why mustn't Gran eat sweet things?
4. Why does Oscar want to babysit?
5. Why can't Oscar hear or see Jake?
6. Why does Oscar make a terrible face before he looks in the fridge?
7. Why do the police think Oscar is the mother when he phones?
8. Say what you think will happen in Scene Two.

Scene Two

Fill in the missing words. They are all in Scene Two:

1. When the police came to the door, Oscar heard a ....
2. The woman in the white car was .... to the hospital.
3. Oscar only sees that the woman's child is not Jake when the child ....
4. Oscar thought the woman was a kidnapper because he has too much ....
5. Oscar feels .... because he is not a good babysitter.

After you have read the play

1. Are these sentences right or wrong? if they are wrong, correct them.
   a. Oscar did all his homework.
   b. Gran didn't eat any cake.
   c. Oscar ate all the cake.
   d. At the end of the play, Oscar still thinks babysitting is easy.
   e. Oscar listened to reggae music.
   f. Gran and Oscar had a very quiet evening.
   g. Oscar saw a woman in a blue coat.

2. What can you say about these words in the play?

upstairs

the fridge

Sleep tight!

skateboard

EDX 181 D

'Kidnapped'

fast asleep

sofa

£1.50 an hour

earphones

3. Think of different ways to *say* these words from the play. What is the best way? (Find the words in the play. Does your voice go up or down? Is it loud or not?)

- *Wow! Lucky you, Oscar! I'm just doing my homework.*
- *I want my Mummy!*
- *Nick! Lucy! Oh! I mustn't shout. Gran will hear!*
- *Now we must tell Gran, Oscar!*
- *Hello! Police! Someone has kidnapped little Jake Wilson!*
- *Huh! Very sorry! Now I'll arrive late at the hospital.*
- *So, who kidnapped him, Gran?*
- *How was Jake? Any problems?*
- *We had a very quiet evening, didn't we, Oscar?*

4. What do *you* think?

a. I like/don't like Oscar because he ....
....

b. The best part of the play is when ....
....

c. If my class acts this play I want to be ....
because he/she ....

Project

Think up a new adventure for Oscar. Work in groups. Write a storyline (= a short text about the story). Choose the best storyline in the class. Then write the story as a play. Act it out in class. You can record it on a cassette, too. Have fun!

Before you read

1. Do you have neighbours? Tell the class about them.
2. Draw the most interesting one and decribe him/her.
3. Do you sometimes have problems with your neighbours?
4. What do you say/do, for example, when your ball goes over your neighbour's fence? Say it in English!

Scene One

1. What is Oscar's neighbour doing in his garden?
2. What does Oscar think?
3. Fill in these sentences with the prepositions *back/ over/out:*
   a. The ball's gone .... the fence.
   b. We must get it ....
   c. I'll climb ....
   d. The neighbour can throw it ....
   e. Let's get............ of here!

Scene Two

1. Fill in the missing words:
   a. Last night there was a .... at the City Museum.
   b. Thieves .... a famous statue.
   c. The statue is over .... old and is very ....
   d. The police think the thieves .... it somewhere in the city.
   e. The museum is giving £5,000 for information about the statue. This is called a ....

2. Why do the police think the statue is in the city?
3. Where does Oscar go with Dad's newspaper? What do you think?

Scene Three

1. Mr Marsh is carrying something from his car. Why does Oscar think it's the statue?
2. Draw what the children see.
3. Say everything you know about the statue of Queen Nubia.

Scene Four

1. What can the children see in Mr Marsh's garden?
2. Oscar thinks that Mr Marsh has a plan. What is it?
3. Why does Oscar want to tell the police on Saturday?

Scene Five

1. The police constables think Mr Marsh has buried the statue. Why do they think this?
2. One police constable has an idea at the end of the scene. Can you think what it is?

Scene Six

1. Why is Oscar sad and quiet?
2. How does he feel at the end of the play?

After you have read the play

1. Who says what? Say when and why.
   - *Oh, Oscar! You and your imagination!*
   - *Old Marsh is probably burying something secret!*
   - *Oh, dear! Another robbery in town. This time it's the museum.*
   - *What will we do with that boy?*
   - *Five thousand pounds! That's a lot of money, Oscar!*
   - *Are you sure?*
   - *We'll be rich! We'll be famous!*
   - *Egyptian statue? No. How much do they cost?*
   - *That gives me an idea ... Quick, Constable. Let's go back to the museum!*
   - *Our Oscar? There must be some mistake!*
   - *Hey! Come back with my newspaper!*

2. Words for people. Who is what?

Oscar
Lucy
Nick
Mum
Dad
The constables
Mr Marsh

surprised *boring* *silly* *clever* *scared* *polite* *sad* *stupid* *angry* *funny* *nice* *strange*

Project

Write the next scene.
Oscar goes to the museum to get his reward. Does something funny happen? Maybe the thieves are there ... .

Answers:

Oscar Goes Babysitting
Scene Two: 1. knock – 2. on her way – 3. turns round
4. imagination – 5. sad

Oscar and the Statue
Scene Two: 1. a. robbery – b. stole – c. two thousand years/heavy – d. are hiding – e. reward